P9-CKC-649

LAKE OSWEGO JR. HIGH SCHOOL
2500 SW COUNTRY CLUB RD
LAKE OSWEGO, OR 97034
503-534-2335

THE MAYAS

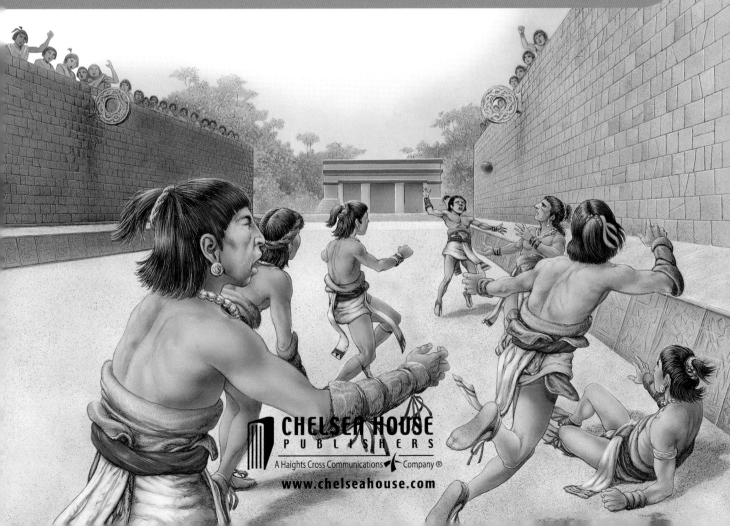

CHELSEA HOUSE
PUBLISHERS
A Haights Cross Communications ◆ Company ®
www.chelseahouse.com

First hardcover library edition published
in the United States of America in
2006 by Chelsea House Publishers,
a subsidiary of Haights Cross Communications.
All rights reserved.

A Haights Cross Communications Company ®

www.chelseahouse.com

Library of Congress Cataloging-in-Publication
Gassos, Dolores.
  The Mayas / Dolores Gassos.
    p. cm.—(Ancient civilizations)
  Includes bibliographical references and index.
  ISBN 0-7910-8489-2 (hard cover)
    1. Mayas—History. 2. Mayas—Social life
and customs. 3. Mayas—Folklore. I. Title.
II. Ancient civilizations (Philadelphia, Pa.).
F1435.G28 2005
972.81'016-dc22
              2005007042

Production and Realization
Parramón Ediciones, S.A.

Text
Dolores Gassós

Translator
Patrick Clark

Illustrations
Marcel Socias Studio

Graphic Design and Typesetting
Estudi Toni Inglés (Alba Marco)

First edition: April 2005

Ancient Civilizations
The Mayas

Printed in Spain
© Parramón Ediciones, S.A. – 2005
Ronda de Sant Pere, 5, 4ª planta
08010 Barcelona (España)
Empresa del Grupo Editorial Norma

www.parramon.com

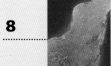

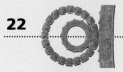

IN THE JUNGLES OF CENTRAL AMERICA

One cannot help but be surprised that a people who did not know the practical uses of the wheel, and did not employ animals either for labor or transport, succeeded in creating one of the most brilliant civilizations in the history of humanity. The Mayas had very limited technology, but they, nevertheless, managed to colonize a major portion of Central America and built numerous city-states. The impressive monuments they built continue to attract the admiration of people today. By the beginning of the sixteenth century, however, when the Spanish conquistadors arrived in the area, Mayan civilization had already begun to decline. It was through the conquistadors that Europe came to learn about the legendary greatness of the Mayas.

This book aims to awaken in young readers an interest in the fascinating culture of the Mayas. After a brief historical introduction, eleven topics, touching on the most important aspects of a culture that endured for more than 3,000 years, are approached by means of text and illustrations. The central image gives the reader an immediate idea of the subject, while the text, which is both informative and anecdotal, supplies essential information about that topic. At the end of the book, there is a chronology showing the main periods of Mayan history, and a brief summary of interesting facts.

THE SPLENDOR OF PRE-COLUMBIAN AMERICA

These glyphs are signs that the Mayas used to designate the days and the years.

THE CORN PEOPLE

The Mayas settled in the area of Petén and the Yucatán Peninsula around the year 1500 B.C. It is not known where they came from, or how they were able to develop an extraordinarily advanced civilization with a political system based on city-states, a well-organized system of administration, a religion of great theological and ritual sophistication, and art of great beauty and perfection. These people lived in the present-day territories of Guatemala, Belize, and southern Mexico, until the arrival of the Spaniards, who established a presence in 1515, but did not completely conquer the area until 1696. By the time the conquistadors arrived, Mayan civilization was already in decline, and most of the Mayan ceremonial centers had been abandoned.

Mayan history spans over an extended period, and scholars have divided it into three major stages:
• Pre-classical, from about 1500 B.C. to 317 A.D.
• Classical, which covers the years between 317 A.D. and 889 A.D.
• Postclassical, which runs from 889 to 1696.

A PROMISING START

The first known Mayan settlements are found in the Pacific region, and date back

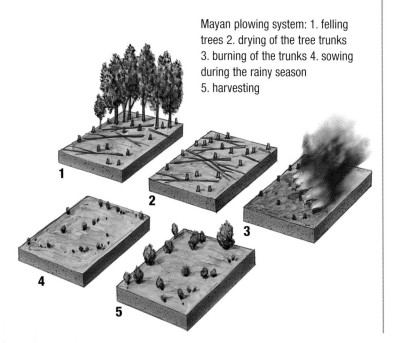

Mayan plowing system: 1. felling trees 2. drying of the tree trunks 3. burning of the trunks 4. sowing during the rainy season 5. harvesting

Image of Tlacatzinacantli, the man-bat.

to a time before 1500 B.C., the year when the Pre-classical period begins. This period, which signifies the beginning of Mayan culture proper, is characterized by the appearance of complex societies, and by the development and expansion of agriculture based on corn. During this period, the Mayas, who had already adapted themselves to the features of their new environment, continued to perfect the art of pottery, and began to create the religious belief system that defined them as a people.

The Mayas were never able to create a unified state. Their political system was based on city-states, large religious and administrative centers governed by a king. Each city-state controlled a large territory, in which representatives of the king governed numerous peasant villages. At times, these city-states fought with each other. Some scholars believe these confrontations caused some of the periods of decline that characterize Mayan history. When the king of one city-state defeated another king, he took as prisoners all of the members of the royal family, and seized all of the possessions of the defeated sovereign. The arrival of the prisoners to the territory of the victor set off great feasts and celebrations, during which human sacrifices took place.

During the Pre-classical period, among the states that reached the greatest heights of splendor and development were Tikal, Copán, Palenque, and Cobá.

TWO GREAT DISCOVERIES: WRITING AND THE CALENDAR

Writing first appeared toward the end of the Pre-classical period. This invention led directly to the Classical period, when Mayan civilization reached its greatest splendor. The two major advances of the Classical period were the development of writing and the appearance of the calendar. These two innovations made it possible for people today to know something about Mayan history. The names and chronological order of the great kings of different city-states have been gathered from stone steles that the Mayans left behind.

Thanks to written information contained in Mayan codices, it has been possible to get to know their traditional legends and religious beliefs. It was during the Classical period that characteristic features of the Mayan world, such as dated stones,

The disturbing jade funerary mask of the ruler Pakal. It was found in the Temple of Inscriptions, in Palenque.

natural causes, wars between the Mayans themselves, or widespread famine. Some believe it may have been caused by the eruption of a volcano in Guatemala. This volcano spewed lava and ashes over an area extending some 25 miles out, and caused great destruction and climatic changes.

Mayan civilization entered into a period of lethargy, not emerging until the beginning of the tenth century, when peoples from the North arrived in the Yucatán Peninsula. They assimilated Mayan culture, and reinvigorated it. New settlements such as Uxmal, Chichén

buildings with projecting limestone vaults, and the typical architectural style that defines this capable and enterprising people, appeared and were perfected. The arts in general reached their greatest period of growth around the year 790, a period that saw unprecedented construction activity. This was when some of the most famous Mayan centers, such as Copán, Piedras Negras, Yaxchilán, Palenque, Calakmul, and Edzná, experienced their greatest era of prosperity.

REEMERGING FROM THE ASHES
Around the beginning of the ninth century, the population of the Mayan region drastically declined. Many city-states were abandoned, and many stone steles were left unfinished. Scholars do not know exactly what caused this sudden decline, which may have been due to

Decorated Mayan pottery vessel.

In this fragment of the Laud Codex, one can see a man seated on the glyph that represents the Tree of Life.

Itzá, and Mayapán, which were the leading cities of the Postclassical period, arose in the Yucatán. The Postclassical period was marked by considerable population density, and a more complex social organization than in earlier periods. Architectural activity regained its old peak, and potters produced vessels of great technical perfection, although less ornamented than in previous eras.

THE DISTURBING ARRIVAL OF THE SPANIARDS

The Spanish landed in the Mayan area beginning in 1515. The Mayas were not a powerful state, given their city-state structure, but in the face of danger, these small independent entities formed alliances to fight invaders, and succeeded in keeping the Spanish at bay for some time. Indeed, the Spaniards made two unsuccessful attempts at conquest in 1527–1528, and again in 1531–1535. When the conquistadors undertook their final attack in the mid-sixteenth century, this time successfully, there were some 18 independent Mayan states in the Yucatán Peninsula.

The leading factor in the ultimate defeat of the Mayas was the personal vengeance of a Mayan king. This deed unleashed a terrible civil war that weakened the Mayan people. Furthermore, some traitors joined forces with the Spaniards, who then returned to the area, and, with great ease, were able to subjugate a people exhausted and decimated by war and disease.

In this way, a civilization capable of organizing solemn religious and civil festivals, and able to construct enormous ceremonial complexes, was destroyed forever. But many of its buildings have survived into our time as proof of the greatness of a people who dominated a large part of Central America for many centuries.

THE YUCATÁN PENINSULA

In about the year 1500 B.C., an indigenous people of unknown origins settled in Central America and went on to create a surprisingly advanced civilization. These people settled primarily in the highlands near the Pacific Ocean, but around the year 1000 A.D., they moved to the plains of the Yucatán Peninsula, where they built their main urban centers. Their lands, now largely covered by tropical forests and crossed by deep rivers, are shared among the present-day countries of Mexico, Guatemala, Belize, and Honduras.

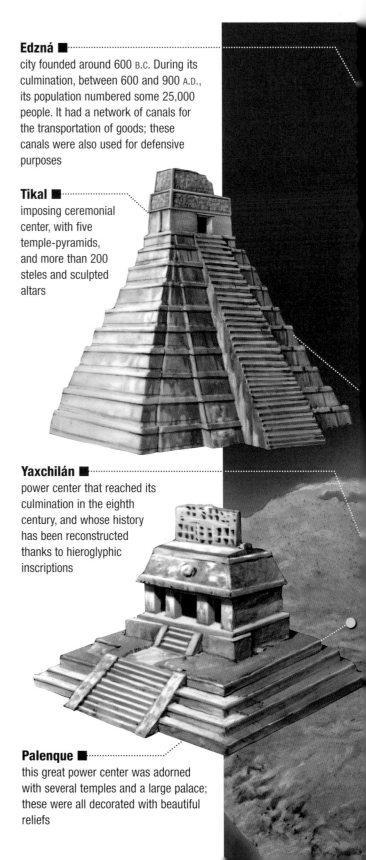

Edzná ■
city founded around 600 B.C. During its culmination, between 600 and 900 A.D., its population numbered some 25,000 people. It had a network of canals for the transportation of goods; these canals were also used for defensive purposes

Tikal ■
imposing ceremonial center, with five temple-pyramids, and more than 200 steles and sculpted altars

Yaxchilán ■
power center that reached its culmination in the eighth century, and whose history has been reconstructed thanks to hieroglyphic inscriptions

Palenque ■
this great power center was adorned with several temples and a large palace; these were all decorated with beautiful reliefs

The tropical forest

The leading Mayan city-states were built in the midst of a thick tropical forest, formed by very tall trees such as mahogany, cedrelas, and palm trees, and inhabited by animals such as the jaguar, the quetzal (a native bird), and the toucan.

CLIMATE OF THE MAYAN AREA

In the area where the Mayas lived, there is constant, year-round heat, and seasons are distinguished only by differing amounts of rainfall. There is a dry season and a rainy season; these marked the rhythm of Mayan life, and had special importance for work in the fields.

Uxmal ■
Impressive city built between the seventh and tenth centuries A.D.; the building facades display rich and varied decorations

■ Izamal
this ancient center of pilgrimage featured a dozen sanctuaries dedicated to the creation god, Itzamná, and to the sun god, Ahau

Chichén Itzá ■
very important and vast ceremonial complex, which was surely a place where sacrifices were offered to the rain god

Labná

Tulum

Sayil

Chacmultún

Dzibilnocac

■ Lamanai
large ceremonial complex located on the shores of the Río Nuevo lagoon. It features a pyramid 115 feet high, outfitted with large masks

Copán ■
this city was built during the Pre-classical period of Mayan civilization, and was known as a center of astronomical investigation

Hochob

Balamku

Becán

Chicanná

Xpujil

Hormiguero

Kohunlich

Calakmul

Uaxactum

Xunantunich

■ Bonampak
small ceremonial and feudal complex that preserves very important wall paintings in the three chambers of one of its temples

THE SAP OF LIFE

The main economic activity of the Mayan world was agriculture, which was carried out on communal lands, and centered on the cultivation of corn, beans, pumpkins, tapioca, cacao, avocados, and tomatoes. Corn, a plant originating in Mayan territory, reached Europe only in the sixteenth century, before spreading all over the world. The sowing and harvesting of this staple plant, a basic element of the Mayan diet, determined the timing of major religious festivals.

■ **tortillas**
the staple food made with corn flour was the tortilla or *tlaxcalli*, a very thin, flat cake that was cooked in a clay container

■ **corn flour**
the flour that resulted from grinding corn was used to make various foods, such as rice cereal

■ *comal*
the *comal* [koh MAHL], a very large clay pot with slightly raised edges, was used to cook corn tortillas

■ **grains**
after removing the grains from the cob, they could be boiled or soaked in water and quick lime to be softened, before being eaten

■ *metate*
softened grains of corn were milled on the *metate* [meh TAH tay], a rectangular stone on which the grains were flattened with a stone rolling pin called a pestle

CACAO

One of the great treasures of the Mayan area was the cacao tree, which grew in Guatemala and in a few areas in southern Mexico. Cacao beans were used as currency because of their great value, and because they could be used to make a drink, which was popular with the elite members of society.

■ *posol*
the Mayas also made *posol* [poh SOHL], a drink very similar to beer, from the fermentation of corn grains

digging stick ■
to cultivate corn, Mayan farmers used digging sticks and various stone implements; they did not know about the plow, and their only domestic animal was the dog

■ **cob**
the fruit of the corn is the cob, which the Mayas frequently consumed after toasting it directly over the fire

BLOODTHIRSTY SPIRITS

The Mayan gods grew out of personifications of natural forces that act on people and their environment. They were beneficent and evildoing gods, who exercised positive or negative influence over peoples' lives. Their interventions were not inexorable in nature, but could be redirected by means of proper execution of rites and sacrifices. The most important god in the Mayan pantheon was Itzamná, the creator of all human beings and animals.

reliefs ■
Chac is the Mayan god most often depicted; his odd face appears on reliefs in many buildings

Chac ■
the long projecting nose of the rain god, Chac, resembles the head of a serpent

eyes and ears ■
Chac's prominent eyes have a human appearance, and the decorations on his ears also look like something people would wear

beneficent divinity ■
Chac was a beneficent divinity who measured out the necessary rain, and provoked atmospheric phenomena such as wind, thunder, and lightning

fangs ■
his mouth, full of fangs, connects him with the jaguar, a mammal that was very honored by the Mayas

THE UNDERWORLD

The underworld, where the sun god wandered around during the night, occupied a very prominent place in Mayan mythology. This was a dark and frozen region, controlled by the gods of death. Wild animals roamed at will there, and sharp knives flew here and there through the air.

■ images

the Mayas did not depict their gods in an anthropomorphic manner, but rather as a mixture of plant, animal, and human traits

■ cardinal points

Chac was depicted either alone or in groups of four, in an allusion to his capacity as god of the four cardinal points

■ worship

worship of Chac, and of the other Mayan gods, basically consisted of celebrations, ritual dances, and animal sacrifices

Corn God

Sun God

Other gods

The Mayas also worshipped other gods, including a sun god, a moon goddess, a water goddess, a god of the dead, and a corn god. Kinich Ahau, the sun god, was a divinity connected with the jaguar, and died and was reborn each day in tune with the solar cycle. Kauil, the corn god, took the form of a young man with a tall headdress formed by open corn leaves.

FROM KING TO PEASANTS

Mayan society was strictly hierarchical. Nobility occupied the top of the social pyramid; this class was composed of families that inherited privileges and responsibilities. Kings, military leaders, and priests, who constituted the social elite, all came from noble stock, as did officials and warriors. The remaining social classes had to earn a living by working, and were obliged to pay tribute to the ruling classes, either in the form of work or in kind. This group included craftsmen, merchants, and peasants.

Warriors

Mayan warriors were descendants of noble families, and received special training. They devoted their lives to the defense of the territory, and to fighting with other city-states in order to increase the sphere of power and influence of their own king.

princes ■
princes, who were second only to kings in importance, were charged with governing towns, carrying out the administration of the state, and important military responsibilities

headdresses ■
all persons of high rank covered their heads with headdresses of great size and enormous complexity; these headdresses had a symbolic meaning

peasants ■
peasants formed the lowest social class; in addition to cultivating the fields, they were employed in public works projects and in transportation

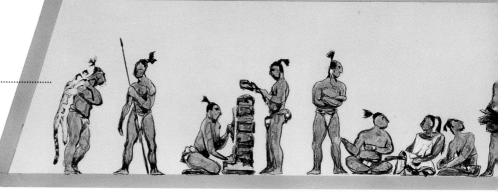

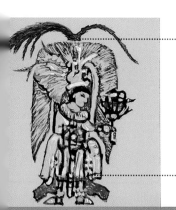

■ **kings**
kings were placed at the top of Mayan society; they enacted laws, chose governors, and made the most important decisions

Slavery was not a hereditary condition, but rather a condition one fell into by being captured as a prisoner of war, or as punishment for committing certain crimes, such as robbery. The main purpose of slaves was to serve as victims for human sacrifice rituals.

■ **attire**
kings lived in large palaces together with their families, and wore beautiful attire on the occasion of solemn ceremonies

■ *manikin*
the stick or ceremonial scepter that high-ranking Mayan dignitaries would wear as a sign of their authority was called a *manikin* in their native language

■ **weapons**
weapons, such as a shield or a lance, were carried as a symbol of power and authority; only the king, princes, and warriors could bear arms

■ **priests**
priests had great power thanks to the influence of their advice and sentences; they were the repositories of Mayan knowledge and science, and presided over religious ceremonies

■ **style of dress**
the style of dress of each individual depended on social class and on the duties fulfilled

■ **craftsmen**
craftsmen belonged to the working classes, but sometimes lived with the nobility, whom they served in a permanent capacity

THE SECRET WORLD OF GOVERNORS AND PRIESTS

Among the Mayas, ceremonial complexes were centers composed mainly of monumental religious buildings. The only inhabitants of these sacred complexes were priests, the kings with their families and court, as well as the servants, and a few craftsmen who worked there full time. The rest of the population could only visit these ceremonial complexes for occasions such as great religious or civil festivals.

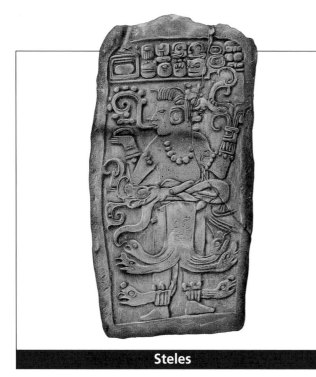

Steles

In some of their ceremonial centers, the Mayas erected large steles made of stone, engraved with portraits of their governors and the dates of the most outstanding events of their reigns. Thanks to these commemorative monuments, long periods of Mayan history are known in detail.

HALLUCINOGENS

The Mayas knew how to use the plants that grew on their lands to produce medicinal products and hallucinogenic substances that the priests consumed in order to enter into a trance for ritual festivals.

spaciousness ■
ceremonial complexes occupied a very extensive area, and were usually located in the middle of the jungle

roads ■
the various buildings were distributed in a haphazard manner, and connected with each other by means of paved stone roads

observatories ■
in some cases, ceremonial complexes were also equipped with an astronomical observatory

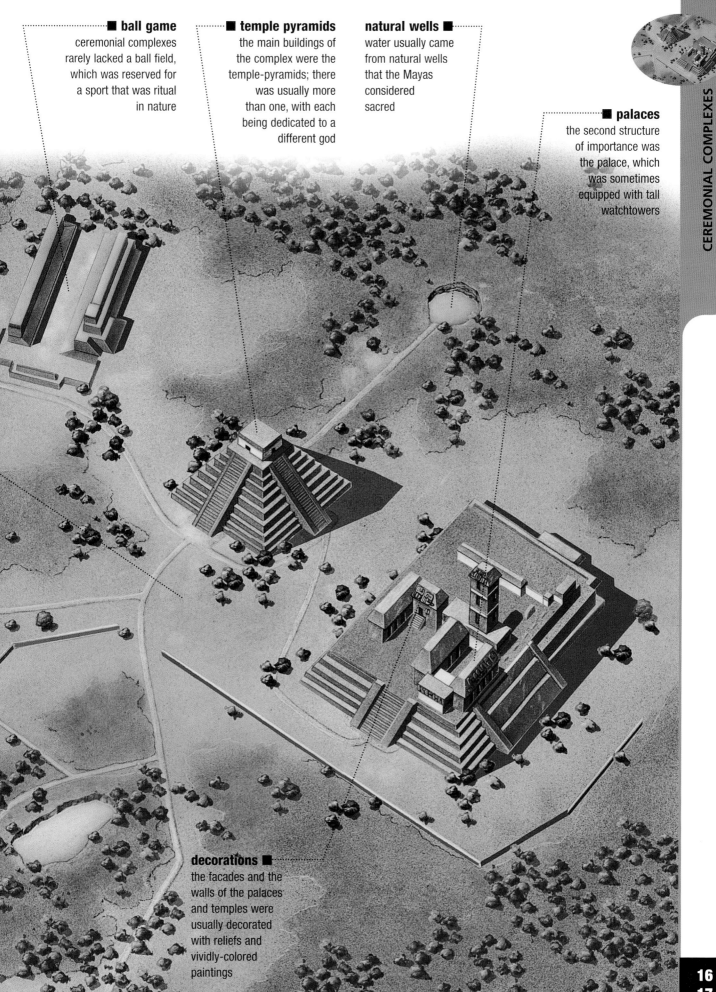

■ ball game
ceremonial complexes
rarely lacked a ball field,
which was reserved for
a sport that was ritual
in nature

■ temple pyramids
the main buildings of
the complex were the
temple-pyramids; there
was usually more
than one, with each
being dedicated to a
different god

natural wells ■
water usually came
from natural wells
that the Mayas
considered
sacred

■ palaces
the second structure
of importance was
the palace, which
was sometimes
equipped with tall
watchtowers

decorations ■
the facades and the
walls of the palaces
and temples were
usually decorated
with reliefs and
vividly-colored
paintings

A SYMBOLIC BUILDING WITH SEVERAL FUNCTIONS

The pyramid was the main building in Mayan ceremonial complexes, and each sacred center usually had more than one pyramid. All of them reached great heights; this was intended to raise the stature of the priests who presided over sacred rites from the top. Sometimes, the highest area of the pyramid was equipped with a small chamber that was intended to amplify the priest's voice so that he could be clearly heard from any point in the complex.

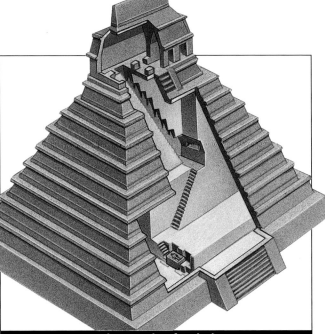

The tomb of Pakal

King Pakal, who ruled in Palenque from 615 to 683, ordered the building of the Temple of Inscriptions, and had his own funeral chamber placed inside it. His body, covered with a precious jade mask, was placed inside a stone sarcophagus with reliefs sculpted on the cover.

platforms ■
most of the pyramids have nine staggered platforms, because the number nine had great importance in the Mayan conception of the universe

"THE CASTLE"

The main pyramid of Chichén Itzá, known as "The Castle," incorporates calendar symbolism: it has 91 steps in each of its four staircases; that number, when added to the single step at the entrance lintel, makes 365, the number of days in the solar year.

stone ■
all Mayan pyramids are made of stone, a material which sometimes covers an interior structure of adobe

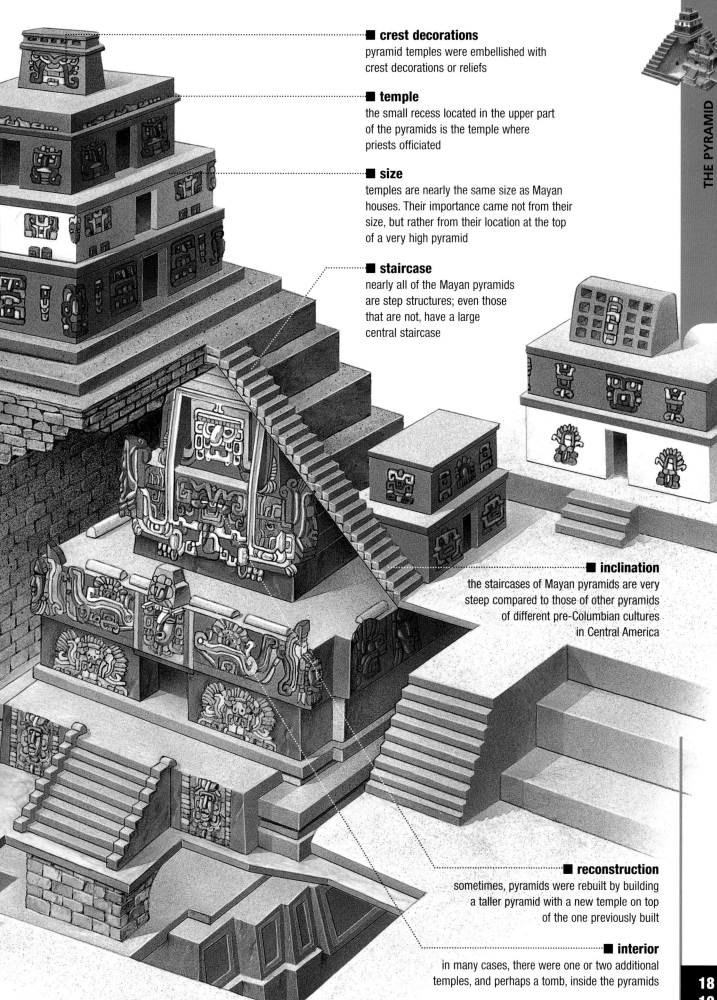

■ **crest decorations**
pyramid temples were embellished with crest decorations or reliefs

■ **temple**
the small recess located in the upper part of the pyramids is the temple where priests officiated

■ **size**
temples are nearly the same size as Mayan houses. Their importance came not from their size, but rather from their location at the top of a very high pyramid

■ **staircase**
nearly all of the Mayan pyramids are step structures; even those that are not, have a large central staircase

■ **inclination**
the staircases of Mayan pyramids are very steep compared to those of other pyramids of different pre-Columbian cultures in Central America

■ **reconstruction**
sometimes, pyramids were rebuilt by building a taller pyramid with a new temple on top of the one previously built

■ **interior**
in many cases, there were one or two additional temples, and perhaps a tomb, inside the pyramids

A SPORT OF LIFE AND DEATH

More than entertainment or a competitive sport, the ball game was an activity of a ritual nature that ended with the sacrifice of the losers. This bloody ritual was practiced by all the civilizations of Central America, not only the Mayas. The exact rules and nature of the game are not known, because the Spanish conquerors did everything they could to wipe out all traces of an activity they considered to be a rite of the devil.

spectators ■
next to the long sides of the field were various spaces where spectators could watch the competition

ring ■
on each of the long sides, there was a large stone ring with a small opening in the center

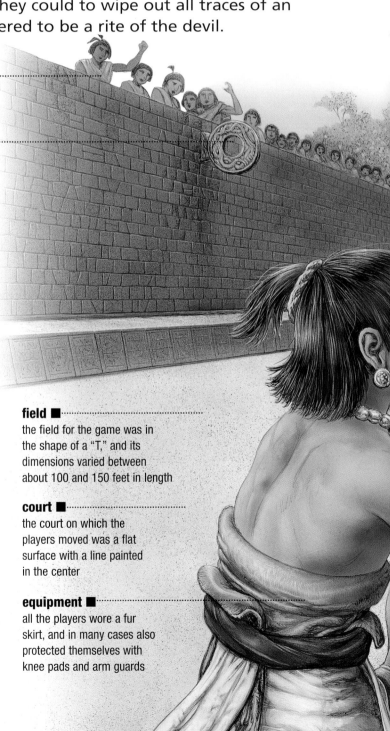

A bloody end

There are numerous reliefs depicting the winners of the ball game executing their rivals; sometimes, the blood of the losers was transformed into serpents or plants, which leads to the idea that, in the final analysis, the ball game was a fertility ritual.

field ■
the field for the game was in the shape of a "T," and its dimensions varied between about 100 and 150 feet in length

court ■
the court on which the players moved was a flat surface with a line painted in the center

equipment ■
all the players wore a fur skirt, and in many cases also protected themselves with knee pads and arm guards

THE BALL

The ball was rubber, almost as big as a human head. It was very large in proportion to the opening it was supposed to go through, and very heavy for the parts of the body that it could hit.

■ goals

the team that got the ball through the ring automatically won the game, regardless of how many points had been scored

skill ■

players tried to keep the ball from touching the ground for as long as possible

touches ■

the players could touch the ball only with their buttocks, hips, or knees; they committed a fault if the ball touched any other part of their body

THE MAYAN CALENDAR

Thanks to their observation of the stars, the Mayas were able to establish a very accurate calendar. The calendar determined the appropriate days for sowing and harvesting, favorable and unfavorable days, as well as the dates for great religious and civil celebrations. These usually coincided with solstices or equinoxes; on such days, priests could impress the public by means of certain light effects that relied on an exact knowledge of the position of the sun.

MAYAN SCIENCE

Although they lacked lenses, watches, and measuring instruments, the Mayas came to understand the phases of the Moon. They were able to predict solar and lunar eclipses, and they knew a lot about planets, such as Venus and Mars. They also had solid mathematical knowledge.

■ **years**
years were designated by the name of the day in the prophetic cycle coinciding with New Year's Day

■ **52 years**
according to this system, the names of years did not repeat until after 52 years passed; this is why the cycle of 52 years was the main chronological unit among the Mayas

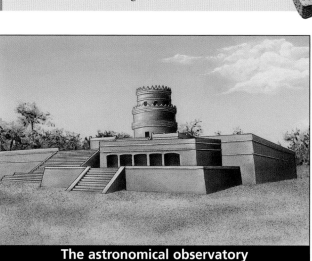

The astronomical observatory

Astronomical observatories were located and oriented in such a way as to favor the observation of the stars with the naked eye, because the Mayas did not have lenses to view distant objects.

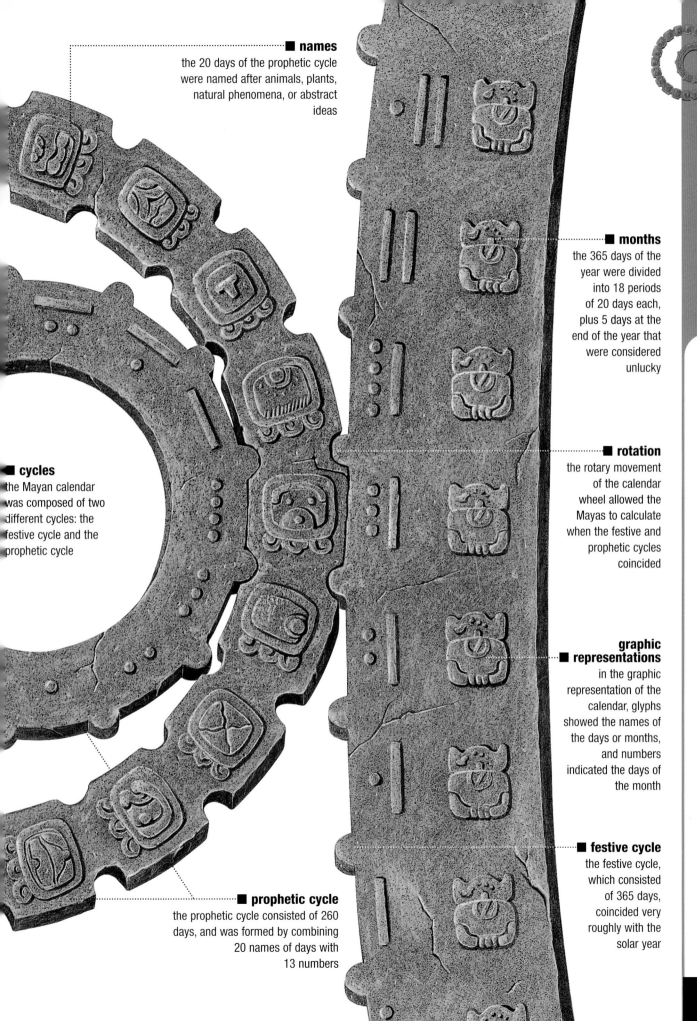

■ names
the 20 days of the prophetic cycle were named after animals, plants, natural phenomena, or abstract ideas

■ months
the 365 days of the year were divided into 18 periods of 20 days each, plus 5 days at the end of the year that were considered unlucky

■ cycles
the Mayan calendar was composed of two different cycles: the festive cycle and the prophetic cycle

■ rotation
the rotary movement of the calendar wheel allowed the Mayas to calculate when the festive and prophetic cycles coincided

graphic ■ representations
in the graphic representation of the calendar, glyphs showed the names of the days or months, and numbers indicated the days of the month

■ festive cycle
the festive cycle, which consisted of 365 days, coincided very roughly with the solar year

■ prophetic cycle
the prophetic cycle consisted of 260 days, and was formed by combining 20 names of days with 13 numbers

ART IN DAILY LIFE

Among all the pre-Columbian cultures, the Mayas reached the highest level of artistic achievement. They carried out more construction projects than other peoples; sculpture and painting developed greatly as arts in the service of architecture; and their crafts were outstanding both for their variety and for the ability of craftsmen to apply their art to the smallest details of daily life. In the Mayan world, crafts and clothing are two closely related concepts.

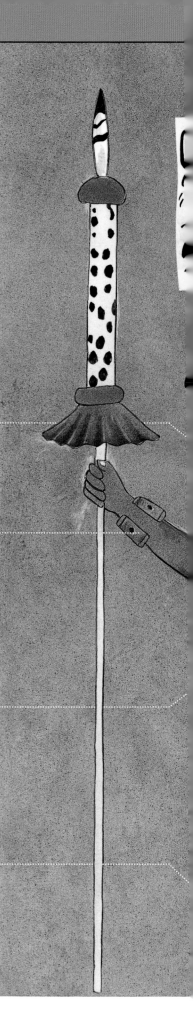

ornaments ■
high-ranking Mayan dignitaries would wear ornaments on their necks, their wrists, their ears, and their shoulders

masters ■
Mayan craftsmen, who worked with jade, obsidian, and other materials such as onyx, diorite, and serpentine, were able to create pieces of great beauty and technical perfection

materials ■
ornaments were usually made either of jade, a green stone that, according to Mayan beliefs, possessed magical powers, or obsidian, a black stone of volcanic origin

sandals ■
sandals consisted of a heel pad and an insole that were bound to the foot by two straps, which passed between the toes and were tied together at the ankle

Seals

The Mayas made seals of clay, or sometimes stone, that they used primarily for the purpose of stamping designs on textiles. Most of these seals were flat, but there were also round ones; these round seals could be used to stamp a continuous series of drawings.

HAIRSTYLES

Mayan women wore their hair long, and styled it in various ways, sometimes using complicated headdresses that hid the hair. Men also wore their hair long, partially trimmed at the top, and collected in a ponytail at the back.

■ **headdresses**
in addition to feathers, Mayan ceremonial headdresses might include animal masks that had a symbolic meaning

■ **feathers**
Mayan head-dresses rarely lacked feathers; these were nearly always the feathers of the quetzal, a bird that was considered sacred

■ **feather art**
feather art, that is to say, the art of making beautiful ornaments with bird feathers, was one of the crafts that the Mayas best understood and cultivated

■ **girdles**
Mayan men normally wore a kind of loincloth or girdle of cloth around the waist; sometimes these girdles extended down to the knees or ankles

■ **skins**
clothing for daily use tended to be made of cotton, which was tinted with various colors, but the Mayas also wore large fur coats on special occasions

THE SIMPLE LIFE OF THE COMMON PEOPLE

The life of Mayan peasants and artisans was very humble. They lived near the fields that they cultivated, in very small houses that they shared with members of their immediate family. There were no clans. Men spent nearly the entire day working in the fields, and women worked occasionally in the gardens, and did all the chores related to food production. The children did not attend school, and began to work from a very young age. In these social classes, no one knew how to read or write.

houses ■
most of the houses were made of *bajareque*, sticks interwoven with reeds and mud, and the roofs were made of palm fronds or grasses

roofs ■
the roofs were angled so that water from torrential rains would slide off, and so leaks would not form

furnishings ■
inside the house, there were only mats for sitting down and sleeping, fabrics to carry loads, and a few pots and wicker baskets

children ■
mothers were busy taking care of their small children, whom they carried on their shoulders in cloth slings

mats ■
the ground inside the dwelling was covered with mats and fabrics to protect against moisture

POTTERY

The Mayas used pottery not only to make articles for daily use, but also to make beautiful little statues of men and women, and ritual containers decorated with complex scenes painted in vivid colors.

■ **clothing**
generally, peasant men wore a simple loincloth, while peasant women wore a loose tunic that came down to their feet

The descendants of the Mayas live today in southern Mexico and Guatemala. They maintain some of the customs of their ancestors, such as the type of dwellings in which they live, the diet based on corn, shoulder straps to carry children, and the tunics that women wear.

The Mayas today

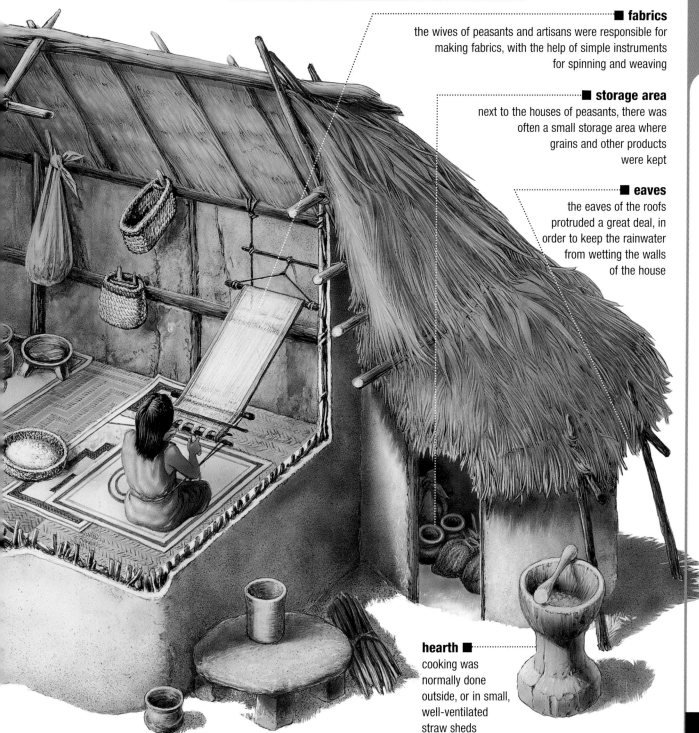

■ fabrics
the wives of peasants and artisans were responsible for making fabrics, with the help of simple instruments for spinning and weaving

■ storage area
next to the houses of peasants, there was often a small storage area where grains and other products were kept

■ eaves
the eaves of the roofs protruded a great deal, in order to keep the rainwater from wetting the walls of the house

hearth ■
cooking was normally done outside, or in small, well-ventilated straw sheds

A SYSTEM BASED ON GLYPHS

The use of writing began to extend over the Mayan territories in roughly the third century A.D. The Mayas used writing in books and manuscripts, but they also wrote on the steps and doors of temples, on steles and altars, on pieces of pottery and ornaments, and on stone, stucco, and wooden tablets. One of the most important Mayan books is the *Popol Vuh*, which describes in the Mayan language the rich Mayan mythology, with its gods and rituals, but uses the Latin alphabet.

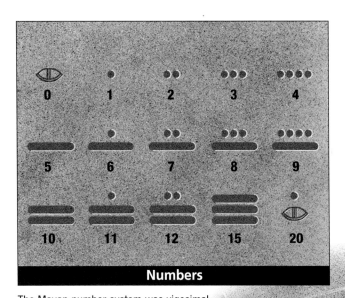

Numbers

The Mayan number system was vigesimal. It used 20 as a base rather than 10. To represent numbers, they used dots for units, and lines for groups of five.

the sacrifice of the god Pakal ■ was found in the Temple of Inscriptions, in Palenque

CODICES

Mayan books, known as codices, were written on both sides of thin strips of bark or skins. The pages were gathered together to fold like an accordion. Only four of these codices survive: the Madrid Codex, the Paris Codex, the Dresden Codex, and the Grolier Codex.

■ **heads**
the most common image in glyphs is a human or animal head, usually depicted in profile

■ **glyphs**
glyphs, the basic elements of Mayan writing, are graphic representations with a syllabic significance

■ **rectangle**
the glyphs are small and rectangular; a main image and several smaller images are engraved

■ **meaning**
a glyph can represent a syllable of a word, an entire word, or a day or month in the Mayan calendar

■ **eight**
the number eight, represented by three points for the units, and a stick for a five, appears in this glyph

■ **mixed glyphs**
glyphs that, in addition to words, contain both syllabic symbols and graphic expressions of numerals

■ **inscriptions of Pakal's sarcophagus**
the glyphs tell us his name, his birth and death dates, and the years of his reign

details ■
in general, the meaning of heads drawn in glyphs depends on small details such as ornaments on the cheeks or the shape of the lower jaw

FURTHER KNOWLEDGE

GREAT PERIODS IN MAYAN CIVILIZATION

1600 B.C.	Pre-classical Formative
1500 B.C.	Early Pre-classical
1000 B.C.	Middle Pre-classical
400 B.C.	Late Pre-classical
100 A.D.	End of Pre-classical or Proto-classical
250 A.D.	Formal Classical
534 A.D.	Middle Classical
593 A.D.	Late Classical
800 A.D.	End of Classical
900 A.D.	Formative Postclassical
1200 A.D.	Late Postclassical
1550 A.D.	Spanish Conquest
1696 A.D.	Colonial

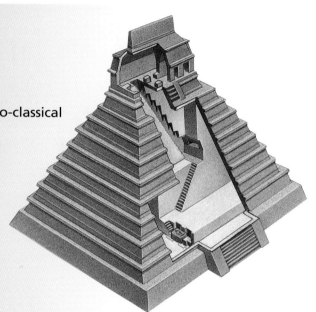

MAYAN GODS

Hunab Ku	He was the only god, creator of the world and of humanity, from corn. He was never depicted. He was the father of Itzamná.
Itzamná	Was considered the chief of the gods. Invented writing books, and the calendar. Was related to Kinich Ahau, the sun god.
Kauil	Was the corn god and the god of agricultural work.
Kukulcán	Was the wind god. He was depicted as a plumed serpent.
Chac	Was the rain god. He was depicted with a nose that looks like a trunk, and had fangs.
Ah Muzenkab	Was the god of bees and honey.
Buluc Chabtan	Was the god of war and of human sacrifices.
Ek Chuach	Was the god of the markets.

MAYAN COSMOLOGY

The Mayas thought of the world as a plane divided into four parts. The base of a pyramid, with its four sides, corresponded to the cardinal points, known to the Mayas as the four "chacs," or rain gods.

Four gods known as *bacabes* held up the celestial vault. Heaven was represented as a two-headed monster, and was divided into three parts, each associated with a particular god. Real life depended on heavenly beings.

The sun god, Kinich Ahau, was one of the most important gods. At his side were the Moon (the goddess Ixchel) and Venus. When night arrived, the Sun went down to the underworld, where he was transformed into a jaguar.

DID YOU KNOW...?

The Mayas

... the Mayas were dark-skinned people of short stature, with heads that were wider than they were tall?

... a green stone called jade had greater value than gold for the Mayas because they believed it had many beneficial magical properties?

... the Mayas energetically hunted and fished to obtain food and furs?

... the Mayas knew of no other method of transportation than the canoe, and people of the lowest social classes would carry merchandise on their shoulders?

... Mayan leaders deformed their skulls voluntarily by using small wooden boards to lengthen and bend their foreheads?

... the apertures in the astronomical observatory of Chichén Itzá indicated the position of certain stars on important dates of the Mayan calendar?

... during the spring solstice, the sun draws the figure of a serpent on one of the staircases of the central pyramid of Chichén Itzá?

... the Spaniards, when they arrived in America, discovered food products such as the tomato, rice, and cacao, that were completely unknown in Europe?

... Tayasil, on the shores of Lake Petén, was the last city conquered by the Spanish, and it was able to maintain its independence until 1696?

... in the *Popol Vuh*, a book that contains the legends of the Mayas, it is said that the creator god made new drinks from corn, and that force and vigor were born from this food, thereby giving flesh and muscle to the first father and the first mother?

Jade mask

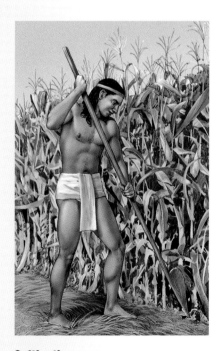

Cultivating corn

INDEX